Rainer

Max Wilkinson

methuen | drama

LONDON • NEW YORK • OXFORD • NEW DELHI • SYDNEY

METHUEN DRAMA
Bloomsbury Publishing Plc
50 Bedford Square, London, WC1B 3DP, UK
1385 Broadway, New York, NY 10018, USA
29 Earlsfort Terrace, Dublin 2, Ireland

BLOOMSBURY, METHUEN DRAMA and the Methuen
Drama logo are trademarks of Bloomsbury Publishing Plc

First published in Great Britain 2022

Cover photo: Max Wilkinson
Graphic Design by India Martin

A catalogue record for this book is available from the British Library.

A catalog record for this book is available from the Library of Congress.

ISBN: PB: 978-1-3503-5092-2
ePDF: 978-1-3503-5093-9
ePub: 978-1-3503-5094-6

Series: Modern Plays

Typeset by Mark Heslington Ltd, Scarborough, North Yorkshire

To find out more about our authors and books visit
www.bloomsbury.com and sign up for our newsletters.

WoLab presents . . .

RAINER

By Max Wilkinson

Writer	**Max Wilkinson**
Director	**Nico Rao Pimparé**
Performer	**Sorcha Kennedy**
Sound Designer	**Jethro Cooke**
Lighting Designer	**Jamie Platt**
Design Consultant	**Zoë Hurwitz**
Stage Management by	**Danielle Harris**
Graphic Design by	**India Martin**
PR by	**Flavia Fraser-Cannon for Mobius PR**

For WoLab:

Creative Director **Alistair Wilkinson**
Associate Director **Kaleya Baxe**

With thanks to: Arcola Theatre, Rikki Beadle-Blair, Johanna Burnheart, Haylin Cai, Sue Emmas, Hannah Kumari, Jerwood Space, Punchdrunk, RTYDS, Holly Adomah Thompson, Lyndsey Turner, the WoLab extended family, and Ian Zarate.

This production was first performed at Arcola Theatre on 1 June 2022

Background from the writer

A monologue partly inspired by Dylan Thomas' *Under Milk Wood* and Mike Leigh's *Naked*, *Rainer* is a love letter to a grimy, beautiful city and its inhabitants: the villains, the saints and everyone in between. But it's also a study of someone desperately in the margins and forgotten.

It was directly inspired by the Covid-19 pandemic, when the streets were apocalyptically clear, save for scores of delivery riders criss-crossing the city. It also draws on my own experience of years of service and delivery jobs and volunteering with Delivery Mutual Aid groups over the pandemic.

More than ever, especially during the pandemic, we relied heavily on delivery people to keep our lives moving, however, most of these workers still blur into the background, regardless of their past or personal story. Rainer is typical of this: highly educated, highly intelligent, half in love with the isolation the job offers, half resentful of it, and in Rainer's case, drowning in her anonymity.

Blending elements of drama and magical realism, it touches on the beauty of the imagination, the danger of isolation and sinking mental health and the people we choose not to see. It's a story that is often ignored, a story that should be told.

Max Wilkinson – Writer

Max is an award-winning playwright fascinated with the characters trying to navigate an increasingly absurd world. He won the Paris Royal Script Award, Screen to Screen Award and was a finalist for the Nick Darke Award, Theatre Uncut's Prize for Political Writing and recently Samuel French's Off Off-Broadway Award. He's also had plays produced at the Arcola Theatre, the King's Head Theatre, Theatre 503, Paines Plough and many others across London. He is currently commissioned to turn his optioned play, *Ghost Fruit*, into a feature film, and his new play *Rainer* will be performed at the Arcola Theatre for three weeks in June 2022, published by Methuen.

Nico Rao Pimparé – Director

Nico is a British-Indian-French director and actor. As a theatre director, he has worked at the Young Vic (Freshworks), the Arcola, the Seven Dials Playhouse, the Bunker Theatre, the Courtyard Theatre, the Blue Elephant Theatre and Theatre N16, receiving critical acclaim. His debut film *The Start of Nothing* recently had its world premiere at BAFTA-qualifying London Short Film Festival 2021, and his feature film *Chaos* is in development with the BFI. He is also an actor, with credits in Hollywood, UK and European TV and Feature productions, as well as theatres across the UK.

Sorcha Kennedy – Performer

Theatre credits include: *Diary of a Somebody* (Seven Dials Playhouse); *Rainer* (Arcola Theatre); *Sam Wanamaker Festival* (Shakespeare's Globe) and *Humbug!* (Citizens Theatre, Glasgow/Tramway). Radio: *Whenever I Get Blown Up I Think of You* (BBC Radio Scotland/RCS). Sorcha trained at the Royal Conservatoire of Scotland and was awarded the Citizens Theatre Society Award for her final performance. She is also a filmmaker and visual artist. Her award-winning directorial debut, *Sisyphos,* starring Leonie Benesch *(The Crown, Babylon Berlin)* is part of the official selection for numerous film festivals in 2022, including Academy Award-qualifying Kortfilmfestivalen.

Alistair Wilkinson – Producer and Creative Director for WoLab

Alistair is a highly experienced, award-winning, queer, working class and disabled artist, originally from Manchester, now living in East London. They trained at Royal Central School of Speech and Drama, as well as on the Royal Court's Invitation Writers Group, and also completed an MA at RADA/Birkbeck. In the past they have made work for organisations such as the BBC, Sky Arts, the National Theatre, the Old Vic, Barbican Centre, Shoreditch Town Hall, Arcola Theatre and Curious Monkey, amongst many others. A lot of Alistair's work focuses on themes of grief, sickness, intimacy and intoxication. They are the former Head of Artist Development at the Old Vic; and are currently leading on all talent development at Punchdrunk, working in the UK, internationally and digitally. They are an Associate Artist at the National Youth Theatre, a Connect Artist for RTYDS, a Trustee for Boundless, and a Script Reader for the Bush Theatre, Theatre Uncut, and The Papatango Prize. Alistair is the Founder and Creative Director of WoLab, and to date, they have raised over £1.77m in funding for various artistic projects.

Jethro Cooke – Sound Designer

Jethro is a composer and sound designer based between Amsterdam and London. He works collaboratively across film, theatre, dance, mime, live art and installed media, combining instrumental and electronic composition to build texturally diverse, emotive pieces and soundworlds. He also builds responsive environments, bespoke instruments, and hardware and software tools for performers. Jethro is co-Artistic Director of Second Body, a multi-award-winning company working with live music and theatre, and runs muon records, an experimental dance music label.

Jamie Platt – Lighting Designer

Jamie trained at RWCMD and has been nominated for a Knight of Illumination Award, a BroadwayWorld Award and five Offie Awards for Best Lighting Design.

Lighting designs include: *The Last Five Years* (West End); *Jellyfish* (National Theatre); *Kes* (Octagon Theatre & Theatre by the Lake); *Cracked, Remembrance* (The Old Vic); *Either, Paradise, Yous Two* (Hampstead Theatre); *The Last Five Years, Beast, Klippies* (Southwark Playhouse); *Anna Karenina* (Silk St. Theatre); *Le Grand Mort* (Trafalgar Studios); *Never Not Once, Gently Down The Stream, Alkaline* (Park Theatre); *Moonlight and Magnolias* (Nottingham Playhouse); *Absurd Person Singular* (Watford Palace Theatre); *The Beat of our Hearts* (Northcott Theatre); *Mythic* (Charing Cross Theatre); *Singin' in the Rain* (The Mill at Sonning); *To Dream Again* (Theatr Clwyd & Polka Theatre); *Blood Orange, The Moor, Where Do Little Birds Go?* (Old Red Lion Theatre); *Checkpoint Chana, Quaint Honour, P'yongyang, We Know Where You Live, Chicken Dust* (Finborough Theatre); *Pattern Recognition* (Platform Theatre and world tour); *Paper Cut, Reared, Screwed, Grey Man* (Theatre503).

Associate lighting designs include: *Disney's Frozen* (West End and International); *INK, The Night of the Iguana, The Starry Messenger, Bitter Wheat* (West End); *SIX* (West End, UK tour and International); *Albion, The Hunt, Three Sisters, Machinal* (Almeida Theatre).

Zoë Hurwitz – Design Consultant

Zoë is a designer for stage and film based in London and New York. In the UK, she has designed for venues such as The Orange Tree, Queens Theatre Hornchurch, The Marlowe Theatre Canterbury, Arts Ed, Jermyn Street Theatre, Hampstead Theatre, Mercury Theatre Colchester, The New Diorama, Shoreditch Town Hall, Warwick Arts Centre, Lamda, The Bunker, The Royal Court and The Director's Programme at the Young Vic. US venues include Here Arts Centre, Ars Nova (AntFest), The Wild Project, The Sheen Center, Colgate University and Brown/Trinity Rep. Selected production design credits include *Assisted Living* (web series, NYC) and 'Pear' (music video, NYC).

Zoë was a winner of the 2019 Linbury Prize for Stage Design and a finalist in the 2020 JMK awards, designing for Emerald Crankson. She has twice been a finalist in the Off West End Awards for best Set Design, most recently for *Deciphering* in 2022. Two of her designs have recently been selected to represent the UK at World Stage Design 2022 in Calgary.

She is a graduate of the MFA Design Programme at Tisch School of the Arts, New York University, and holds a BA in Fine Art from Chelsea School of Art, University of the Arts London.

Credit: Cleo Valentine

Arcola Theatre

Arcola Theatre was founded by Mehmet Ergen and Leyla Nazli in September 2000. Originally located in a former textile factory on Arcola Street in Dalston, in January 2011 the theatre moved to its current location in a former paint-manufacturing workshop on Ashwin Street. In 2021, we opened an additional outdoor performance space just round the corner from the main building: Arcola Outside.

Arcola Theatre produces daring, high-quality theatre in the heart of East London and beyond. We commission and premiere exciting, original works alongside rare gems of world drama and bold new productions of classics. Our socially engaged, international programme champions diversity, challenges the status quo, and attracts over 65,000 people to our building each year. Ticket prices are some of the most affordable in London. Every year, we offer 26 weeks of free rehearsal space to culturally diverse and refugee artists; our Grimeborn Festival opens up opera with contemporary stagings at affordable prices; and our Participation department creates over 13,500 creative opportunities for the people of Hackney and beyond. Our pioneering environmental initiatives are award-winning and aim to make Arcola the world's first carbon-neutral theatre. Arcola has won awards including the UK Theatre Award for Promotion of Diversity, *The Stage* Award for Sustainability and the Peter Brook Empty Space Award.

Twitter, Instagram and Facebook: @arcolatheatre

WoLab

WoLab is a working laboratory for artists to create. They provide performance makers of all experiences with the opportunity to have a go. WoLab trains, mentors, nurtures and creatively entitles artists, helping them discover and refine their talents, and then showcases those talents to the industry. Current work in development includes: *ENG-ER-LAND* by Hannah Kumari, touring to 30+ venues throughout spring/summer 2022; *Rainer* by Max Wilkinson, opening at Arcola Theatre in summer 2022; *Screwdriver* by Eve Cowley and Elin Schofield, recently workshopped with Sheffield Theatres and Sheffield Royal Society For the Blind; *A nightmare is witchwork* by Billie Collins; *In the Net* by Misha Levkov; *A Romantic Comedy* by Tiwa Lade; *TIGER* by Tom Kelsey; *Ostrich* by Alistair Wilkinson; and *The Director's Development Fund*, in partnership with Hannah Joss and Stage Directors UK. Past work includes: *First Commissions* (Paines Plough); *The Actor-Writer Programme* (Theatre N16/Bunker Theatre); *Man-Cub* (RADA/King's Head); *PlayList* (King's Head); *happy ever after?* (Bunker Theatre); and R&D's of *heavymetalsexyanimal* by Sam Rees (Theatre Deli); *Asperger's Children* by Peter Machen (Trinity Laban); and *We'll Be Who We Are* by Naomi Obeng.

Twitter and Instagram: @WoLaboratory

Acknowledgements

For my mum and dad.

And for the invisible people we always see.

And thank you to Mark Hall and Covid Delivery Mutual Aid Groups for having me and talking with me. Thank you to Nico Rao Pimparé and Alistair Wilkinson for making it happen.

Rainer

(A one-woman show)

Character

Rainer

Late twenties/Early thirties. Lower-middle class, British – any ethnicity. She is bold and compassionate, curious and cowardly; best described as a cynical romantic.

Stage Design

*Interpret staging any way you like but recommended would be very minimal or no set with more emphasis on lights and music to elevate the story. **Rainer** should also be wearing her Angel Deliveries outfit; give her lots of room to move around the stage.*

Music

*Music is very important to the piece, simulating **Rainer**'s constant and frenetic movement across the city. This again can be interpreted any way you like but the recommended style would be a blend of euphoric and tragic/sinister electronic music with ghostly echoes of old nostalgic jazz and soul songs occasionally, as this is what **Rainer** listened to with her father. Music like Burial, Aphex Twin, Nina Simone and Ghost Box are good references.*

1

Waterloo.

London.

A warm summer's night as people happily roam around, filling the bars or sitting in parks after work.

Rainer, *who works for Angel Deliveries, stands on a dark stage in her red, lycra coat and her delivery box with Angel logo upon it: white wings.*

She sways to the music slightly, watching the station and the scene from the park.

'La Vie En Rose' by Louis Armstrong or some similar old jazz song plays, but distorted electronically.

Rainer *smiles.*

Hi there, hello.

Nice to see you. Thanks for coming, to a play about me.

Weird that you'd do that but you've paid now and that big door is locked so you can't leave.

Unless you're asthmatic. Or a racist. Then you can go.

Any-hoe . . .

settle in and let me tell you about the worst thing that ever happened to me.

It was last summer. On a night like any other.

Bombing round Waterloo, 6 o'clock and the bars explode.

A man screams at the top of his voice: 'It's coming home!' as a couple kisses by the light of the Tescos.

People were calling it the Summer of Love: the pubs burst with laughter and the parks were strewn with lovers, quietly fucking.

Everyone was fucking.

Even Matt Hancock was fucking.

And after the Lockdown year of watching that potato-faced git on the telly, it was very much deserved.

It was heaven, madame. Until it wasn't.

But how did it start . . .

Oh, yeah, that morning.

There I was, hungover as hell, ready to descend into a wanky hole of cheese toasties and whodunnits when my email coughed up something awful:

'Hello, Rainer, this is your bank: you're basically fucked.'

And indeed I was . . .

Which was odd, cos in my mind I'd been charging round, racking up that cash.

But my account begged to differ.

So, tonight I had to make it up.

Up to Waterloo and get my first ping like that.

Korean place down the road.

Was just here actually, with my brother, for a Bao and a battering.

'When you gonna sort your life out, Raine?' says he, blue suit and Kim-Chied, sitting near the door.

'You're not twenty anymore, it's not sexy.'

'And what is?' I say, almost throwing chilli in his face, 'selling flats to posh twats?'

He leans back and smiles, 'I need you, Raine.'

Cross the bridge: the river breathes.

'Watch out, Rainer!' A few Angels whizz by: that's Angel Deliveries, the company.

There's Qwesi from Botswana, Keri from Cork. Then me.

The nowhere girl. Now, look, I've worked every kind of job.

Bars, cleaner, brief stint at Thames Water, that was weird; but to me, it's all the same.

As long as it pays the bills and I can spy on people.

Cos some guys listen to music, some guys like to sing. I like to work people out.

Anyway, take the Dim-Sum up to those posh flats by the shore.

Some lad waddles out, half-pissed with Friday's pints.

'Hello, mate,' says he, 'how you doing?' Then he grabs the bag and leans in:

'Hey, listen . . . fancy coming in for a bit? Just watching a bit of *Bake Off* with my girlfriend.

You'd like her: she's a solid 8.'

Solid 8 comes screaming to the door and whacks him back inside like a cow.

'You prick!' she turns to me, all bangles and smiles, 'Must be the weirdest thing you've ever seen!'

'No!' I tell her of sex parties and old celebs in Notting Hill who invite me in for tea.

'Oh, wow,' purrs she, then takes my arm . . . 'Listen. We're just watching a little *Bake Off* and if you'd like to –'

And off I fucking go!

Outside their high-rise, London spreads out like Blade Runner.

You can almost see the spaceships. A man stares at me from the bus-stop, then quickly walks away.

Then I get that feeling.

Lights change: white, bright lights of a doctor's office.

'Dissociation' is what my counsellor, Nadia, calls it.

We meet every week in that hospital over there.

'That feeling you get, when you're not really there.'

And look, I know I'm lucky to get a counsellor on the NHS but Nadia, she is quite shit.

'And how's your cystitis?'

'I haven't got that.'

'Oh . . . well, how's everything with your dad?'

'Oh, not great.'

'No?'

'No. He's dead.'

. . .

Dad died of something I can't pronounce.

In a room I don't go in anymore. Anyway, time for a drink.

Her phone pings. Club music plays: 'Voyage, Voyage' by Desireless. Lights go blue, strobe. **Rainer** *dances.*

Soho. Some club called the Clock.

Got a sandwich for the manager, Darren.

The room is covered in writhing, beautiful people.

A fashion party, I think. I mine-sweep shots until someone suddenly tugs at my cloth.

'Oh, my God!' says a beautiful girl, 'Service Chic! I fucking love it.'

Wait, no . . . she doesn't . . .? She does!

She drags me over to a table of other beautiful people and introduces me as a shit-hot designer. Tequila is ordered.

I go for it.

'But who are you?' they ask, beautifully bemused. I invent the wildest lies: fashion shows in Milan, summers in Cannes.

We move to the dance floor. Warm beautiful bodies become one.

I'm about to close my eyes when, across the room, there's someone staring.

Looking. Reaching out for me . . . and then –

'Excuse me,' says an angry little voice: the manager's voice. Darren.

'What you doing out here? Where's my fucking sandwich?'

The whole club is silent. I find my box. I give him his sandwich.

'Wait,' asks a beautiful person, 'so you're not a designer?'

'No,' smiles the manager, 'she's no one.'

. . .

Rainer *stands at the river. She allows her foot to hover over the water.*

. . .

Outside by Battersea Bridge, the sky throbs purple with a little morning.

The water is blue. Inviting . . .

I climb up the stone and stand right on the edge.

. . . Imagine . . .

'Don't do it!'

'What?'

There's a little man in the dark, holding a camera.

'Don't jump!'

'. . . And why not?'

'You've got so much to live for.'

'. . . and how do you know that?'

'. . .'

Just then a cloud passes from the moon and I see his face all bright.

It's a nice face . . .

The kind of face you want to sit on.

'Anyway, what you doing here, you some kind of sex pest?'

'No,' he laughs. 'God no . . . I wish! . . . no. I'm working on a series, about London.'

He lifts his camera but I don't see.

Cos on Battersea Bridge there's a man in a trench coat. Staring down at me.

Staring.

'Are you OK?'

'. . . do you believe in ghosts?'

'Sure. Especially in London. Sometimes . . . sometimes it's hard to breathe.'

And just at that moment, Battersea Bridge lights up like a Christmas tree.

Bright lights shine in a line in the dark.

Trench coat disappears.

I turn to him.

'. . . What did you say your name was?'

'I didn't: Jack.'

2

Rainer *lies asleep in her bed and wakes up, smiling, to sun. She sits and takes a notebook from somewhere.*

The next day it's sunny.

Blue light flickers through the hall.

I do a bit of writing.

I never told you, did I, but I'm a writer. It's about you lot really.

See, I'm using you, you're not using me.

By night I ride, by day I write. All the time. Cos as Bukowski said: you got to go all the way.

So it's a kind of book. I've sent it to all the publishers but . . . no reply.

Thing is, it needs structure. I need help. I need . . . Phoebe Waller-Bridge.

She's not here tonight, is she? No, didn't think so.

I am kind of glad though, you know, cos honestly, you can't move in this town for Waller-Bridges.

I was at Sadler's Wells the other day, right, fan of contemporary dance as *I am* and I'm queuing up for this dance thing, all excited, and I look at the poster and it says: 'music by *Isobel* Waller-Bridge.'

. . . who the fuck is Isobel Waller-Bridge?

. . . Wait, she's not actually here, is she? Don't wanna get whacked.

Or Lloyd Webber coming round.

A crash in the flat.

Suddenly, back in the flat, there's a crash from the shower.

Naked footsteps charge furiously down the hall.

In comes Skyler, my flatmate, wet as a baby and holding something rubbery.

'Can you not leave your fucking Moon Cup in the shower, please? I slipped and nearly broke my bloody neck!'

'Sorry, babe. Must have slipped out.'

She settles down into our greasy sun-lit kitchen and devours some Ryvitas.

'Good night?'

'Oh, amazing. Vauxhall, tons of fun. How was yours?'

'Good, yeah. I met someone.'

'. . . What?'

'What?'

'What, like a *man*?'

'Yes, a *man*.'

'No, that's great, I just thought you might end up like one those women who mutter on buses and smell of wine. Talking of –'

She grabs a vinegary Oyster Bay from the side. 'Bring Jack to the show tonight.'

Oh, no, her show!

Skyler paints colourful concentric circles which I love. That's the line.

'Yeah, sure.'

'And Raine . . . there's someone there that's going to change your life, so best behaviour, yeah?'

I turn to the window as she starts riffling through some letters on the side.

. . . there's a man on the wall. Holding a trench coat.

'Hey, Skyle?'

'Mmm?'

'I think . . . there might be someone following me . . .'

'Like who? Southwark Council? Student Loans?'

'No –'

But as I turn she comes across a particularly horrible letter, stamped with EVICTION.

'What the fuck?'

Shit, was meant to bin that.

'Wait –'

'You're two months late with the rent. How are you two months late?!'

'It's fine!'

I grab the letter and run.

'Rainer!'

'I'm going to sort it!'

Down the stairs as she screams at the top.

But I would sort it.

See in two days it was pay day.

All I had to do was cross the city a million times, plump up that cheque, and all would be fine.

Outside the door, in the New Cross sun, I find Jean there, waiting.

Jean was my beloved bike, named after Jean Rhys, my favourite writer.

I saddle up and wait for a ping.

. . . but nothing. Nada.

Angel App. Dead. Again.

She shakes her phone.

Why did this keep on happening!?

Just when the screen was meant to be covered in hungover, blue dots it suddenly . . . wasn't.

Blank.

Dead.

Her phone pings.

. . . And can you see him over there?

Her phone pings again.

But no! It was fine! Drifting into Peckham, about to despair, the App bursts into life!

Lights change.

'Sama Nanzale' by Pedro Lima plays. **Rainer** *moves to the music, simulating her movement across the city as she delivers.*

Chicken wings and chips.

The queue to the chicken shop vibrates as some men dance and sing in the park.

Take the hot gristle to some posh house near the tracks.

A man in pants waddles out, hungover as hell, grasping the chicken like a child.

'I'm a vegan!' he squeaks, 'But not on Saturdays!'

Then it's burgers in Brockley.

Falafel in Penge.

Then Erol, 'Sweetness!' one of the good ones.

Erol is ancient and lives on a Dulwich Street now solely occupied by shops called Wiggle Piggle.

To curb the tide of gentrification, he visits this place frequently and does violent poos.

'Listen, Rainer,' he chirps from his chair, 'see that bag over there?'

'What, that bag of your old pants?'

'Yeah, put them in the wash!'

'I'm not your pant girl, Erol. I'm just here to eat your pie.'

Every Saturday I bring him a pie and listen to his old jazz records. Ones Dad used to like.

But today, Erol doesn't touch it.

'What's wrong?'

'I don't know . . . today . . . everything's off.'

. . .

Lights change. Bright, clinical lights of a hospital room. Beeping.

'Hello Rainer. How are you?'

Forgot my two o'clock with Sigmund Freud.

'Yeah, really good actually. Brain's like a frickin' fortress right now – no, a house. Yeah, a house with gates and CCTV and big alsations.'

Shut up!

'. . . .Wow. And those pills I gave you?'

'Oh, yeah, great pills, really nice.'

'. . . So, no more panic attacks?'

'No.'

'Black outs?'

'Nope.'

'No more crying on the bus?'

'Only for a treat.'

She leans in.

'. . . And you're not . . . seeing things?'

'I never said . . . I never said I was seeing things I just . . . –
this job is repetitive, you day-dream.'

She sighs.

'Rainer, that feeling you get, the dissociation . . . – we
dissociate to remove ourselves from reality, because
something happened.'

'What happened, Rainer?'

Ok, so recently I decided I didn't want to live anymore, so I
cycled to Beachy Head to do a Quadrophenia.

Now, little tip, if you want to top yourself: don't do it on a
spring morning in South-East England.

Birds were singing, brooks babbled. It was disgusting. Barely
made it past the M25.

Nadia leans in.

'I didn't mean that . . .'

. . .

Lights change to orange and **Rainer** *holds a package, smiling but
horribly uncomfortable.*

I am doing amazingly well.

By 4 o'clock I've served all of south London with grease and
mayonnaise so I heard north.

To greener plains. Camden, Hampstead, leafy streets.

To a particularly lovely house in Golders Green, with a
tiramisu.

I knock on the door.

And think about Jack.

About his pretty little face. Maybe I'll take that face to Margate and sit on it all day.

Then waddle down to the sea. And drink beer by the shore.

'Rainer?'

. . .

'Rainer, is that you?'

Oh, fuck.

'Hey, Finn.'

My ex. Who I'm definitely still in love with.

'How you doin, Raine?'

'Yeah, really good actually, yeah. Just doing this for research.

'Yea, I'm doing a Louie Theroux. I'm doing a book and it's going to be published in the Fall. I mean Autumn, Autumn.'

'Right . . .'

Something squeaks behind him. Something in a pram.

'Oh . . . who's this little . . . sack of potatoes –'

The baby shoots me a look: who the fuck are you?

'Funny, Finn, actually, yeah, cos you said you never . . . wanted kids.'

'Oh, yeah, well I guess . . . something just clicked.'

The *something that clicked* comes running to the door.

'Babe, the plates are getting cold.'

She stops. Smiles. Impossible to hate.

'Who's this?'

'Rainer, yes, we –'

'We used to –'

'We used to –'

'Know each other.'

I just ride away.

Lights change. **Rainer** *sits and takes a beer from her delivery box.*

Well, after that I obviously need a big drink.

Take some tinnies up to the Heath and watch the city shrink.

Angel Apps gone dead again anyway . . .

Me and Dad used to come up here. After some really bad fights.

She sips her drink.

God, I do love drink. I'm not an alcoholic. I just love beer.

And as Baudelaire said: 'Be drunk. Always. Whether it's wine, poetry or virtue, be drunk. Or life will break you.'

Dad told me that quote. He was a writer, famous too.

And by ten the whole city's drunk.

Ping.

Suddenly the app pings into life. Screen flooded with blue dots.

So I take Jean and descend.

Down to Shoreditch where the City boys scream.

Their ladies trotting past.

Essex lads cry and laugh in a deadly dance of Doner meat and displaced love.

In Hoxton I pop into a party to deliver limes.

Some PHD students sway over long white lines and discuss the need for radical change.

It starts to rain.

The white light of a car's headlight shines on her and gets brighter and brighter.

I cross the city a thousand times.

Bringing burgers to stoners still up.

To bad dates.

Mascara running.

Office execs, high up in The Shard.

Lovers in duvets suddenly hungry.

I'm there.

Like an angel they bless me as I stand at the door.

The car's headlight gets brighter and brighter and a horn sounds which gets louder and louder.

Money pours.

In little vibrations. 4 quid a time.

Money pours as the streets blur back and forth.

Back and forth.

Tomorrow I'll write this all down.

Back and forth.

Tomorrow.

But tonight.

Tonight, I'm in love.

She rides into the back of a car.

*The car beeps and swerves as **Rainer** screams and crashes to the floor.*

She falls to the ground and lies there for a moment.

A voice is heard:

'Rainer.'

She looks up . . .

'. . . Dad?'

. . .

. . .

She picks herself up slowly.

Bright lights. Sounds of people talking politely. Skyler's Private View.

'Ce'st La Ouv' by Caroline Loeb plays. She's dazed and confused but regains composure.

'Are you bleeding?'

'Um. Maybe.'

Skyler's private view.

Beautiful people roam around her in concentric circles, saying beautiful things.

'You could have at least changed!'

'Sorry, had to come from work.'

She sighs but then points to the crowd.

'See her, over there?' She points to an evil girl in a jump suit.

'Yes?'

'That, my friend: is Zaza Bones.'

'Who the hell is Zaza Bones?'

'She's a shit-hot publisher, don't be rude. I told her about your book. She's semi-interested.'

'Semi?'

'She's Austrian. She shows little-to-no emotion. It's a big deal.'

'I don't want a big deal, Skyler. I want peanuts. I want to mingle.'

'. . .'

'. . . you don't want me to mingle?'

'No! Of course, just . . . don't go on about awful shit like Jean Rhys and Climate Change.'

She grabs me.

'Just be your lovely old self, OK? . . . But just . . . lovelier.'

She pushes me into the crowd, where I fall, head first, into someone's pink DMs.

'Rainer, right?' a voice hisses above: Zaza Bones.

She extends a scaly hand.

'I heard about your book, sounds interesting.'

'Thank you.'

'And it's based on you?'

'Sort of. Um . . . it's more about the people I meet. Who I deliver to, and –

'And do you fuck these people?'

'I'm sorry?'

'Do you eat them? Do you kill them?'

'No –'

'I'm just trying to find an angle.

'See, we publish books that break boundaries. Cross genres. Break taboos.'

'Right.'

'Are you breaking taboos?'

'Um, not currently.'

A sad waiter drifts by with crudités. I take one and nibble.

'See, I guess, what it is, Zaza . . . my book . . . is about people. Sort of celebrating . . . people. And the city –'

'But why? People are dull?'

'Well . . . I don't think they are?'

'Well, you're not a publisher. Are you?'

'. . .'

'Look, if I wanted to know about people, I'd take the tube.'

'And when did you last do that?'

She leans in and smiles, eyes thinning.

'Look bitch. I only did this as a favour. I have no interest in you or your silly book about hobos. So, just play nice, OK?'

. . . I look down at the crudité. Some goat's cheese mess.

'What are you doing?'

I lift the crudité –

'What are you doing?!'

I press the crudité.

'AHHHH!'

Right into her stupid, little face.

'WHAT ARE YOU DOING?!'

'What's the matter? I thought you liked cheese?!'

The whole room erupts.

Zaza goes berserk.

'AHHH!'

Skyler runs in, all smiles.

'Don't worry everyone: it's a performance!'

Then turns to Zaza: 'Sorry, babe, she's autistic.'

Then to me.

'What the hell are you doing?'

But I'm gone. 'Rainer?'

Out to the street.

'RAINER!'

Cars flash by in a river of red.

'RAINER!'

Pushing past a man in a trench coat, I swerve into the road.

I tell you what, ladies and gents, there is a war going on.

Between fuckers like that and fuckers like me.

Fuckers like that who prance in galleries and do a little poo and sell it for gold.

And fuckers like me. With a little integrity.

Who sweat in little rooms or sweat out here to make something that will never see the light of day.

'RAINER!'

It's a war. The same war waged between those high-rise flats and the little ones down below.

Between the cranes that pick at the sky and the guy who sleeps in piss at the bottom.

It's a war: and they're winning.

The cars swerve past her and beep. 'Theme from Countryman' by Wally Badarou starts to play.

Cross the street to some clubs down the road.

Scary bouncer beeps my head with a covid gun. 'She's clear.'

Descend to the basement, low room, limbs flailing.

Music is good.

Warm faces. I dance with them.

Shedding my shameful outfit.

Emerging like a butterfly.

. . .

She smiles and dances.

Someone dances close.

A man.

A man in a trench coat.

. . .

The music fades away. We hear a voice as the man walks towards **Rainer**.

She is terrified.

To audience: Staring at me.

Can you see him, staring?

Can you see?

Grab the bouncer by the door but he's ear-plugged and blank.

Oh, god, he's walking now.

He's reaching out!

Blocking the door, I can't . . .

'Rainer . . .'

I can't get out!

'Rainer!'

'I can't . . . –'

She cowers on the ground, covering her face.

'Rainer?'

She turns back around: it's Jack. The music starts to build again.

'Jack!'

But it's not him. It's Jack. Jack.

I hold him like a cat.

'I saw you in the street, I shouted –'

I kiss him.

Like I've never kissed anyone before.

Like it's the last time. Even though it's the first.

His body's tense. But then it loosens. Then we sway.

And the walls fall away.

. . .

Lights change but the music continues, 'Theme from Countryman.'

On the night bus back home, people dream.

Heads pressed against the glass, they dream of trees and falling from them.

Of bruised knees and places far away.

'Nearly there.'

Me and Jack dream too.

And talk. Of books and films and secrets never said.

Of the things we'll do, and things we've done.

'Nearly there.'

We kiss and cross the river, water rising.

Back home we tumble up the stairs.

Into his room, sheets lit gold as the dawn approaches.

Lying there we stop.

And look.

Then peel everything back.

And kiss, everything.

And as we become one something happens.

Something I have never felt and I will never feel again . . .

No more words. No more fucking words.

Just me.

And him.

And that's it.

That's it.

3

Sunlight.

Birds sing.

Rainer *happily opens her eyes and looks over at her bed but finds it empty . . . she finds a handwritten note from Jack and smiles, remembering.*

Next morning I wake at Jack's place.

But no Jack. A note though:

'Sorry had to work at the cafe on the hill. Meet me later in Waterloo, at the Three Bells.'

. . . the Three Bells . . . hmm.

My phone vibrates, an email:

A publisher?! No. Angel Deliveries.

'Hi, Rainer. This is Samantha, there's been a problem with your app –'

I'll say!

'Please come in immediately so we can talk.'

No way.

Day off today.

I leave Jack's and demolish a Greggs in the park.

Where am I? North? East?

Suddenly, from the trees, a very pissed off Skyler approaches.

'You're an absolute cunt!' she says, brandishing a tinny G and T.

'Wait, what are you doing here?'

'You called me, you big dummy. Asked to meet.'

'. . . Oh yeah. But why am I a cunt?'

'Because you ruined last night!'

'Oh, come on –'

'No! Zaza was in bits. People were *confused*.'

'Oh, babe, look,' I take her hand and sit. 'Zaza. She doesn't love you. But I do, I love you.'

'Urgh,' she grips her hungover head.

'. . . And I think I'm in love with Jack.'

'You can't be in love. You only met him yesterday.'

'That's long enough.'

'It's really not.'

She says, snorting something naughty from a tube around her neck.

Ah, but what does she know: she doesn't know love, she just knows ketamine.

'Anyway,' she chirps, 'I've just been bollocked by Greek Phil: we need to pay the rent. Today.'

'I know –'

'Seriously, Raine. He's got the courts involved –'

'It's fine, babe!' I pat her little head.

'Cos tonight I'll be paid and all will be well.'

She looks at me.

'What? I've been working all the time.'

'. . .'

'What?'

'Well, just . . . you have been quite forgetful of late.'

'Says you!'

'Why?'

'Cos you brain's like a sieve.'

'It is not . . . sieve-like.'

'What day is it then?' I sip her G and T.

'Um. Tuesday.'

'No, it's Thursday.'

'I meant Thursday.'

'Well, it's not, it's actually Tuesday.'

'Oh, fuck off!' she grabs her forehead again and sucks the G and T.

I smile. 'Look, don't worry, Skyle, it's fine. I'm in love and it's pay day and everything's gonna be fine.'

She takes my hand. Eyes water a little.

'Just remember, Raine.'

'. . . Remember what happened.'

. . .

'Power' by TSHA plays and **Rainer** *dances to it whilst speaking.*

. . . But I don't want to remember. I want to be here. Now.

I leave old sour pants in the park and walk out down the street to . . .

Dalston! Yes, I knew I was north.

Dalston is kicking off. The market swells.

Pubs burst and spill across.

People key powder and vibrate with cans and hold hands up to the sun.

That's London: when it's good, it's the best.

Like when you're in love.

When you're in love, the dust at the bus stop dances in the breeze.

The fag ends are confetti.

The dreadful public art at Tescos is a metaphor for everything.

Jack hasn't texted but that's fine.

We know where we're meeting.

I find myself in an alley, near the canal.

Squat little houses all in a row.

Jazz song from the beginning of the show plays, 'La Vie En Rose' by Louis Armstrong or something similar.

Mum lives here, actually, in Bow. Well . . . I might as well.

'Hi, Mum!' I enter my childhood home. Or the valley of screams as I call it.

'Where you been?' I find her sat down in the sitting room. Playing Scrabble with herself.

'I've been texting; calling.'

'Sorry . . . had a lot on.'

'*Facebook* is not a lot on.'

' . . .'

' . . .'

' . . . How's the garden, Mum?'

'Overgrown.'

' . . .'

'I might . . . go upstairs. For a bit, Mum.'

'Ok.'

Upstairs by the toilet, there's that room where Dad did all the dying.

Still smell the fags.

His trench coat hanging on the door.

'Rainer.'

You ever seen someone die?

They disappear in front of you.

'Rainer.'

I remember one day, he drew me in, gaunt as fuck. Beneath that old, French Noir poster. *Le Samourai*.

'Rainer, listen. Remember: you gotta go all the way.'

'You might lose friends. Your job. Even.

'But if you're gonna go: go all the way.'

I don't go in.

Dreamy music plays but later becomes distorted.

I go home, grab Jean and ride to Waterloo.

The Three Bells.

Outside the pub the sky growls as people rush to the station.

I have a negroni to steady my nerves.

Not that I'm nervous.

I knew I knew this pub.

Actually, I got dumped right over there. Remember Mr Tiramisu?

'It's not me, it's you.'

Funny how the ghosts build up. I see him take my hand:

'I love you. But you don't love yourself.'

Well, that's a crock of shit: I love myself. I'm one of my own top five favourite things:

Tea, lube, the films of Alain Deloin.

'Negroni please!'

He's late now.

People are looking. That man by the fire . . .

'Yes, mate. You alright?'

He's fucking late now. He's really late.

I call him.

It's too loud.

Go outside.

Sky heavy and fat with rain.

Cracks and throbs. Ready. I call him. Text. Crack. I draw up his WhatsApp.

But his little picture's gone.

He hasn't.

Has he? He's –

Lights change.

'Ghosted you . . .' I can almost hear Skyler's annoying posh, little voice.

'What's ghosted?'

'It's when someone fucks you and leaves you.'

Lightning, rain, thunder. She looks up.

The sky above Waterloo finally cracks.

Thunder splits the sky and rain falls down in sheets.

People scream and run to the station, covering heads in soggy Metros.

'He fucked you, then he's left you.'

'But he wouldn't do that!'

'Why?'

'Cos he's . . . – you know he's –'

'What? Sensitive, clever? Says profound things?' –

'Yes.'

'Well, he's a Soft Boy, then –'

'What's a Soft Boy?'

'Jesus, how are you this out the loop?'

'Just tell me.'

I drift down Lower Marsh.

'It's when someone pretends to be all intellectual and arty but actually they're just a big, fat twat.'

The rain comes down in sheets.

'Just like everyone else.'

I stop outside a vintage shop.

I see pictures in the window pane:

Margate. Jack. Chips by the sea.

All slip down like wet sand.

'Excuse me?' says a tiny voice behind me.

A pretty student girl, with a card machine.

'You forgot to pay?'

'Oh, right, sorry.'

Rainer *taps her card on the card machine. It doesn't work. She does it again. And again.*

'Think it's your machine.'

'Probably not,' she squirms, 'it's new. Maybe it's your card?'

How dare she.

'Maybe it's your strip?'

How dare she insult my strip.

'Where are you going?!'

I am not going to stand here and let my card be insulted by some first year!

'Oi!'

I take Jean and just ride right away. The waitress shouts and people stare! 'STOP!'

I ride to the river.

Roaring grey against the side.

Poplar, Limehouse; then go North.

Stratford. Don't know why.

The Olympic Bowl and the marshes thick with reeds.

Beneath a bridge, I check my account.

They never paid . . .

No money. No man. Nothing.

And the Angel App is dead.

Why is it dead?! Why?

A duck drifts by. Quacking like a maniac.

I think of Jack.

'Are you alright?'

'Are you OK?'

There's an American man on the bridge. Against the moon.

'Jesus, you're shivering.'

'. . .'

'Listen, my place is . . . pretty close, if you wanna warm up?'

. . .

Lights change and she lies down on the floor.

His flat smells like potpourri. Empty boxes.

'Just moved in,' he tells me, handing me a towel and a whisky.

'It's too sterile, though. Don't like it.'

I laugh for some reason: 'HAH,' and look outside to the gleaming flats of Stratford.

Spaceships.

Tears in the rain.

'I work in the city,' he says, pouring more whisky, 'but don't hold that against me.'

I *do* hold it against him.

'What do you do?'

'I'm an Influencer.'

'Of what?'

'. . .'

He's handsome.

In a Patrick Bateman kind of way. He tells me about his parents' farm and the fields and how suffocating and lonely a place London can be.

And then he touches my knee.

Then kisses it. I let him.

We lie back on the couch. He peels my clothes away.

Lights flash. She hears the sea and Jack's voice. She sits up.

'Rainer!'

She jolts up.

Jack?

'Rainer! Can you hear me, are you there?'

She looks around.

'What's wrong?' says American face.

'What?'

'Are you OK, where are you going?'

'Gotta go.'

'Why?'

'Cos I don't know you and you're creepy and I want to.'

He smiles.

'Let's just talk then.'

'No.'

He grabs my arm. I pull away. He pulls me down.

'You're lonely, aren't you? I'm lonely too.'

'Get-off!'

'Just stay.'

Rainer *is dragged to the floor and held there.*

He climbs on top of me. Drags me down. There's a stool nearby. IKEA, I think.

'Just stay!'

I grab. The leg. And swing it. Full force.

Filling his face with cheap, Swedish MDF!

'Ah, fuck!' blood bursts.

He screams as I run.

Out the door, down the stairs.

'BITCH!' he screams at the top, 'BITCH!'

As I ride out from Stratford. And into the day.

Lights go black.

Rainer *lies on the floor. Looking up. Lights slowly fade up. Morning. Grey. Rain outside the window.*

4

And then it rained. It rained forever. I watched it from my window.

Ducks swam down the New Cross Road; Wales was subsumed.

And inside me something grew.

At first I thought it was gas.

Or a hangover long overdue.

But no . . .

It was the C.

SFX: COOOOOOOOOOVID and lights flash.

Covid! The Big Catherine! I'd eluded her this long but now she sat firmly upon me.

And I don't mean mildly. No loss of taste and ginger tea.

It was shaking nights and dripping walls and chest as tight as fuck.

'Skyler!' I croaked on Day 2.

'Skyler, I know you hate me but can I have an apple, please?'

Nothing.

Day Three and the room shook like a ship.

I even try Jack. Voicemail.

'Hi there, I know we don't really know each other but there is a tiny, tiny chance that I might die so yeah, if you could call me back at some point that would be really great.'

But nothing.

Day Four and a knock at the door.

Knock, knock, knock.

A plate of Ryvita and a note: 'you're still a twat,' Skyler! 'but don't die.'

By Day Six the Ryvita starts to speak: 'Eat me, Rainer!' it says, flapping away on the plate, 'you need to eat!'

'But I can't, Ryvita.'

'But why?'

'Cos you're too dry, I told you!'

'But I'm covered in almond butter!'

'I know, but I can't swallow a thing.'

Thunder and rain danced on the wall.

On Day 8. Jean Rhys comes to visit me.

Sitting on the end of my bed in an excellent hat.

'Hello, Rainer. How do you do?'

'Oh, Jean, please, not now!'

'But why, my dear?'

'Cos you're my hero; and I'm just in this horrible hole!'

'You call this a hole?' she scoffs, 'this is bloody Christmas to me!'

'Anyway, I did my best work in holes. Bed-sits in Plymouth; suicidal as fuck.'

'But that's what I mean, Jean!'

'I'm just not depressed enough to be a great a writer!'

She squeaks, 'Well, thank your lucky stars, my dear!'

'Do you think I wanted to be depressed all the time?'

'But your books –'

'So?'

She nibbles some Ryvita on the plate.

'I would have honestly traded every word for a slightly more blissful life.'

She adjusts her hat.

'But Jean, what about Bukowski?'

'What about him?'

'He said you gotta go all the way!'

'Yeah, but he was a bit of a twat, wasn't he?

I live with him actually, in this kind of Purgatory flat.'

'Oh, how's that?'

'Um, not bad. Good facilities.'

. . .

Then she jumps out the window, 'OK, bye!'

'But Jean!'

Lighting lashes against the glass.

Something cracks. Breaks against the floor.

'AHHHH!', I scream as I step back through broken shards.

Back into the duvet. Cover face and shake.

. . .

. . . But then . . .

. . . there's someone there.

Someone else.

Is his long trench coat.

He sits on the bed. Puts a cool hand on my head.

And for the first time.

I let him . . .

Storm subsides.

. . .

. . .

But on Day 10.

It stops. Sunny. Blue clouds. And a knock at the door.

And it's . . . it's . . .

'Jack!'

All pale and beautiful; I hold him like a cat.

'Come on!'

He grabs my hand and we rush to Victoria.

Take the train.

Two hours to whisper. No need to explain.

Of books and dreams and one day, a place by the sea.

And then Margate, Dreamland. And chips by the beach.

And the words:

'I love you.'

Then tumble into bed.

The sounds drift away. She is in her room.

5

Rainer lies on the floor as the storm subsides and morning comes on. Birds sing. Sun shines through the window. She lifts her head cautiously.

But no.

Just my room.

Ryvita. Broken glass.

A note from Skyler: 'gone to Mallorca, need to clear my head.'

Great.

Another eviction email.

And Angel Deliveries. 'Rainer, you need to come in. It's about the Ap –'

But then . . . something else.

An email. From a publisher!

'Rainer! We've read your work and we love it.'

Oh my God, oh my God!

'You're incredible! Unique!'

. . .

But no. Just the normal mix of rejection and mails about ED.

I haven't even got Erectile Dysfunction.

Knock on the door.

'. . . Jack?'

Another knock. She runs to the door.

'Jack?!'

No.

An Angel. Like me.

'Rainer Williams?'

She holds flowers. Her small hands quivering in her red coat.

'From Jack.'

Jack! Jack! I could kiss her little face.

There's a note with the flowers.

'Waited for you at the Three Bells, Rainer . . . don't know what happened.'

'What?'

'I hope I haven't got it wrong.'

What are you talking about?

The Angel girl has already fled down the stairs.

I grab her from the top.

'Wait? Where are these flowers from?'

She looks scared.

'Please, I'm one of you!'

. . .

'Finsbury Park.'

. . .

I ride to Finsbury Park, Jean's grinding gears rusted from the rain.

Long lines of red houses. But which one was his?

Can't remember.

Angel HQ calls again.

'Please Rainer –'

'Fuck off!'

My eyes drift to the cafe in the park. On the hill.

He said he worked in a cafe, didn't he? Yes! In the park!

I run down the street and up the hill, punching through mummies and whippets.

The cafe is covered in plastic: a murder scene with scones.

'Hello!'

A big posh lady taps my head with a Covid gun. It flashes red.

'Oh . . .' she staggers back.

'No, it's not Covid, it's um . . .'

What?

'Cystitis. It's cystitis; I'm currently riddled.'

'Oh'

'Quite embarrassing, really –'

'Shoosh.'

She puts a finger to her lips,

'Please. I am a fellow sufferer: I'm flaring up as we speak!'

I smile.

'Great, listen: you don't know a Jack, do you?'

'Um.'

'Weedy? Tall? Sad eyes like a cow?' She squeals,

'Oh . . . yes, Daisy! He used work weekends. He left.'

'Do you know where he lives?'

'. . .'

'I'm basically his . . . cousin and, um, we went raving but he ran off and now I'm worried he's selling his ass down the Holloway Road.'

Nice.

She stops. And thinks. Then finds a battered CV behind the til.

With an address at the top.

'Oi!'

I grab it and run.

. . .

His house looks different. Smaller, grottier.

My hand freezes at the bell.

In a park with a pond, some kids smoke skunk on the bench.

A swan drifts by.

'Oi, I dare you slap that swan, fam,' says one boy on the bench.

'Why am I gonna slap a swan for?'

'Why, you a pussy? You think it will break your arm?

'I'm not a pussy, jus . . . it's illegal, innit.'

'What?'

'They're owned by the Queen.'

'Shut-up!'

'They are!'

'So, what, the Queen's gonna jump out the trees if you slap it?'

'No, but police might.'

'. . . You're a pussy.'

Just then a light flickers on at Jack's.

Fuck it.

She rings the doorbell. The door opens.

'Hiya! . . . Oh.'

At the door is the drunkest, saddest woman I've ever seen.

'Hello, I didn't order anything?'

'Um,' I rummage through my bag. Find a tiny Scotch egg.

'I don't even like eggs . . .'

A smoke alarm sounds in the kitchen. 'Shit!' she hurtles back in. I follow.

A greasy student kitchen filled with *Peep Show* quotes and black smoke.

'I've burnt my fucking chips!' she throws a black pan and collapses in tears.

I fill her glass with Echo Falls.

'What's wrong?'

She's so sad. So Northern.

'So, I went on a Hinge date, right. Fucker called me a Cat Fish!'

'Why?'

'Said I had deceptively fat arms!'

'No, no, your arms aren't fat! They're small, if anything.'

'Thanks. I have two dates a day, you know. One in the evening, then a Pret Matinee.'

'Why?'

'Cos I got to get out of this hole! Meet someone, you know.'

Fresh tears ensue. I stroke her hair.

'Listen, you'll be fine: you're hot, you're nice, you've got perfectly proportioned arms: all will be well.'

'You think?' she's drifting away.

'Listen, when will Jack be back?'

'Jack, yeah. He . . . lives here.'

'No, we're all girls here.'

She's drifting away. I shake her.

'No, but I was here!'

'What.'

'I was here, just the other day!'

But she's gone. Head lolloped forward. Drifted away.

I creep upstairs. To sticky hall and bare light bulb.

'Jack?'

I open a door; then another, then another.

Sequins. Perfume. Photos on the mirror.

. . . He was never here.

And neither was I.

. . .

Lights go bright white.

'Rainer. Can you hear me?'

Nadia's voice.

'. . . Yup.'

'I know you haven't been taking those pills, Rainer. Because you think they numb out.'

. . . but listen.

'If you don't take them.

They can lead to mania. Amnesia. Depression. Hallucination. And then. Maybe . . .

'What?'

. . .

Lights go red. **Rainer** *drifts to the West End.*

'Hi Rainer, so good to meet you.'

Angel Deliveries calls again, so I drift down to the West End.

Into a room of cushions and mirrors.

My apparent boss, Samantha, sits in the middle. Sanitising her hands.

'Sorry, I'm a bit nervous. It's like meeting the Queen. Or . . . Lana Del Ray.'

'Really?'

'Yeah – I'm just so sorry you've been having all these problems with your, App!'

'Samantha,' bashful as fuck, 'these things happen.'

'They don't. Not at Angel Deliveries.'

Here we go. Champagne please.

'I just can't believe the App kept on going. Even after we terminated your account!'

. . .

'What?'

'The Angel App. Kept on giving you work –'

'When did you terminate my account?'

'. . . We emailed you.'

'I didn't get it.'

She grabs and swipes a tablet.

'Yeah, here we go. June the 10th – for *inappropriate behaviour.*'

'What *inappropriate behaviour?*'

'Well, there's a lot –'

'Like what?'

'Apparently every Saturday. You eat . . . a pie. With a man in Dulwich.'

'He pays for the pie.'

'The pie's not the point, Rainer. You're meant to *give* him the pie. Not help him to consume it.'

'Yeah, but –'

She swipes.

'And look at this: the other week you were meant to deliver a sandwich to a man in a club but instead you "danced like a lunatic, pounded shots and tried to pass yourself off as a fashion Designer from Milan".'

'. . .'

'Are you a Fashion Designer from Milan?'

'No, but . . . – it's not my fault you make us so damn stylish!'

'Why didn't you tell them, then? I got calls from Dolce Gabbana! Louis Vuitton. People were very confused –'

'Yeah, but –'

She swipes.

'You helped a woman with her plumbing?'

'She was frail –'

'Played chess with a gravedigger.'

'After hours –

'Had a bath with the Mayor of Camden.'

'That was . . . – a mistake.'

She sighs.

Her tablet flashes.

'And look! This just came in now! You stroked a girl's hair in Finsbury Park, tonight!'

'How you getting this?'

'Reviews, Rainer. Reviews:

'*Angel . . . Delives are real sick. Not only dus Rainer bring da scotch eggs she also brings da cuddles. I hope she finds her friend, Smack*'

'Yeah, but look at all those stars!'

'It's not the point, Rainer. We're not some sexy Task Rabbit!'

'I don't get sexy.'

'Well, you did a few weeks ago. Down in Bermondsey –'

'What?'

She swipes.

'Rainer is very punctual. And very hot. She brought the Dim-Sum but sadly didn't stay for the *three*-some. Maybe next time.'

'See! I walked away. Even though his girlfriend was a Solid 8 –'

'Rainer!' she snaps.

Then sanitises.

'Look. This job . . . can put us in . . . *difficult situations* sometimes.' –

'I'll say.'

'But we have to draw the line. Right down the doorway!'

A water machine gurgles.

'You do not' and reads: 'help people with *political decisions*.'

'She was running for mayor!'

'Or help film Jewish weddings!'

'They were down a DP!'

'Or call the managing director of the Tate Modern a Flaming Cunt!'

'He was . . . a very . . . rude man.'

. . . We breathe.

She sanitises. I stand.

'Look. I get it. You've got a business to run. But Sam. May I call you Sam?'

'No.'

'Samantha,' my voice rising.

'I know I don't do things by the book. I know I don't always follow the rules –'

BAFTA please.

'But answer me this: if there is no room in this company for a little compassion. Then what kind of a company are we?'

'. . . A highly profitable one.'

'One that, I'm afraid, doesn't need your, um . . . *unique approach*.'

'. . . Right.'

I fall back to the cushions.

The machine gurgles.

'So I'm fired?'

'No. You've been *released*.'

. . .

I look round the room for sharp objects.

Something to break that mirror. But it's all so damn soft.

'Is that why you do it here?'

'What?'

She doesn't hear, she swipes.

'But wait . . . if you didn't know you'd been released –'

'I was still taking jobs, yeah, so I better be paid.'

'Of course,' she shows me the tablet.

'. . . Two hundred pounds?'

'Two hundred and *twelve* pounds.'

'For *two months*?'

'Where you made a total,' she swipes, 'of: 57 deliveries.'

'But I make that in a day!'

'Which day?'

'Any day. Last week.'

'Which one?'

'August 8th. Check that. On your little *thing*.'

She does. Fingers dancing like a spider.

'Here we go. August 8th.' She shows me a map, 'they're the blue dots, you're the red.'

She shows me a small section of Hackney where a depressingly small amount of blue dots cover the map.

'. . . But. I remember that day. I went everywhere –'

'Rainer –'

'It was really nice. We'd just had all that rain and then everyone thought the summer was done –'

'Listen.'

'And then everyone was out. On the canals, and the River Lea. And they were all happy. And . . . and . . .'

'Sounds like a lovely day.'

She stands.

'My dad died.'

'What?'

'Yeah, that's why I couldn't take so many deliveries.'

'I see.'

'I had the funeral.'

'Of course!'

'But the others one I did them, I did them.'

'. . . Rainer.'

I bury my head in a cushion.

'Maybe, you should . . . see someone?'

'What, here?'

'No, the NHS –'

'No. Done them –'

'Well, then I'm sorry –'

'Are you?'

'. . .'

'Are you really?'

She eyes the door.

'Cos that's the thing with you lot. When you join it's all: *'hey, be your own boss: be a frickin' rock star!'*

'But when your dad's dying, you don't want to bloody know!'

She reaches for her phone.

'I have been spat on, jeered at, left out in the rain for this job.'

'Leon, come quick!'

'And just because I try to show a little . . . *warmth*.'

'Leon.'

'You throw me to the dogs.'

I'm in her face now.

'Cos Samantha, this isn't just work, for me, right? This is my life.'

'LEON!'

'This is my LIFE!'

She screams down the phone as I grab it out her hand.

Hurling it across the room, it twists and shines black in the heavy, white air.

Curving like a stone as it lands bang in the middle of the mirror.

The wall shatters.

The room breaks.

Leon comes in.

Everything falls.

. . .

6

'Compensation' by Nina Simone plays, a gospel tune.

I lock up Jean and ride the bus home.

Rattling down the Old Kent Road.

Everyone's faces against the glass, dreaming.

Of tax returns and awkward dinners.

Of things said badly.

Of a beach somewhere . . . someone holding a towel.

There's a woman singing, on the seat ahead.

'Sorry? What song is that? It's beautiful.'

'I dunno. My dad used to sing it. I don't know its name.'

'Funny that,' I lean back. 'So did mine.'

. . .

Rainer *bangs at the door of her apartment on the busy New Cross Road, looking up towards the fourth-floor window and her flat. Traffic sounds.*

'Phill!'

. . .

'PHILL!'

. . .

'Phil, I can see you in the window, mate!'

A grimy window of my flat flings open. Greek Phil pops his head out.

'What's up?'

'What's up?! You've locked me out.'

He shakes his massive head.

'Rainer, mate, I warned you.'

'But –'

'I'm sorry, OK?'

'What about my stuff?'

'It's over there, in that bag.'

He points to a hiking bag and a couple of totes.

I grab it and charge into the road.

'You got somewhere to stay?'

'Don't worry about me, Phil, I got plenty of places to go!'

'3' by Aphex Twin plays or similarly ambient, darker music.

Note to self: I have nowhere to go.

Skyler in Mallorca, Jack has flown.

Mum . . .?

No.

The Old Kent Road swims.

Boy racers scream past, high on nang gas, dropping silver pellets by the lights.

'You, alright?' someone asks me as I swerve past the Tescos.

'Yeah, fine.'

Unlock Jean . . . no, Jean's gone. Soho, I left her.

'You OK?'

'Yes, I'm fine!'

It starts to rain.

Find some greasy old coins in my bag and buy an awful bottle of wine.

She sits down and starts to drift away.

Sit by Burgess Park.

Beneath some trees.

Start to drift.

The road.

Blurs.

'That road will kill you,' Dad used to say.

Can almost hear him.

Smell him.

That old trench coat.

. . .

. . . I

. . .

I . . .

. . .

I hear. Light. Footsteps. Approach.

Her eyes slowly widen and open in horror as she sees the Man in the Trench Coat approach her.

Lights go red. Music gets more intense and builds from here.

'Rainer.'

'No . . .'

'Rainer!'

No!

There he is, can you see him? Oh, god.

'Rainer, please!'

Staggers forward like a drunk. Grey coat flapping.

'Rainer!'

'Leave me alone!'

I have to go. Run.

Run up the hill.

Down to the Rye.

Trees split in the dark.

'Rainer!'

Somehow in Dulwich. A quiet street.

Erol . . . Erol lives here!

Do you remember Erol? Sweet Erol, who eats a pie.

I find his house and see him sleeping there.

She bangs on the glass of **Erol**'s *house.*

'Erol!'

Warm face, eyes about to open.

. . . But they don't. They don't.

'Erol! EROL!'

His mouth. Not breathing.

'EROL!'

. . .

. . .

'Rainer.'

No!

See him there? In the bushes?

'Rainer!'

Street lights flicker. I can see his face . . .

'Please . . .'

I run.

I run.

Down the Walworth Road.

To Waterloo.

The river.

Beating at the side.

Find a tunnel. Hide.

I hear Nadia's voice in the dark.

'Rainer, listen.'

'. . .'

'You see him because you won't face it. Won't face what happened.'

'Nothing happened!'

I see him again. In the tunnel.

Fine, cross the bridge.

A car swerves past her.

'Kaneda's Theme' – From Akira Soundtrack – plays and builds as cars swerve past her, tourists and all manner of awful things.

Down to Soho. Spring rolls and Selfie sticks.

Tourists and teens.

'Smack him up!'

Suddenly, a line of Hare Krishna shuffle past, orange dongs and incense.

'Rainer!'

'No!'

She runs and kneels down.

She looks up at the moon in Trafalgar Square and closes her eyes.

Trafalgar Square.

Stop. Breathe. Blue.

Moon.

This . . . Jean! I find her there. Locked up in the dark.

I kiss her metal frame.

I kiss her like a cat.

. . . Then there are faces.

'Oi, bruv, is she crack?'

'Please.'

'Oi! She likes you, man!'

'Nah! Man, she's nasty, shut up.'

'Oi, take her bike.'

'No!'

'Go on!'

'NO, PLEASE!'

She claws at the boys to get her bike back but the boys run away, laughing.

. . . A protest screams.

Climate Change I think.

'OUR HOUSE IS ONE FIRE,' they scream.

'IT'S ON FIRE. AND YOU DO NOTHING!'

Crawl into China Town.

Red lanterns bob.

In market stalls. There's . . .

Someone hunched.

Over a bowl of noodles.

In a trench coat.

He turns to me.

'Rainer.'

'NO!'

'No!' I run, through the crowds, through people. 'WATCH OUT!'

Lights against her; cars, swerving and beeping.

Cars scream past, lights.

'WATCH OUT!'

And Trench Coat stands.

He takes a gun from his heavy brown coat.

And he kneels.

And he shouts, 'WATCH OUT!' and the crowds clear.

So he can have a nice shot.

He kneels.

He shoots.

Then . . .

. . .

. . . Black.

. . .

A car hits her head on.

Red and white lights.

She lies on the floor.

She lies on the floor for some time.

Blue lights flash dimly against her.

. . .

. . .

7

. . .

'Hello?'

'Are you OK?' . . .

A woman is tapping me in the leafy dark.

'You're in my garden.' And sure enough, there I was, sitting in her roses.

'I've got a delivery for you,' I say, clambering for my box.

'But I didn't order anything.'

She's right. My box is empty. She smiles.

'Would you like a glass of water?'

Her house is nice.

Full of old things.

Books. Pictures. A large, brass owl.

'I like your owl. Must have been expensive.'

'Yes.'

She hands me the water. She has big, sad eyes.

'Do you live here alone?'

'No.'

She turns.

'Yes. I . . . – now I do.'

She points to a picture. A smiling man.

'My husband died last summer.'

'He was a lot older than me.'

'He was . . . he was the only person I could ever talk to . . . I mean . . . without thinking first, you know?'

'I do. I had someone like that.'

'Where is he now?'

'. . . He ghosted me.'

The clock ticks.

'Can I ask you something?'

'Of course.'

'When you coupled up with him, your husband; weren't you worried about him being old? About him . . .

'Dying?'

I nod. She smiles.

'No. Rainer, life has such little joy: If you find some. Hold on to it.'

. . . And then I just fucking cry.

Hot salty, snotty tears.

I cry like a little girl.

And she just sits there. Until I'm finished. Then takes my hand. And smiles, and says:

'Keep going, Rainer.'

Bright lights. Bleeping. White room. '4' by Aphex Twin plays lightly and builds.

A hospital room.

London. Lights.

My whole body tied up to tubes.

Skyler . . .?

'She's awake!'

She squeaks, red faced by the vending machine.

'How do you feel?' Nadia too?

'Where am I?'

'St Thomas's. They found your medical card, they –'

Rainer *tries to sit up but it's very painful.*

'No, don't sit up, don't sit up.'

Rainer *eases down again.*

Skyler shuffles up. Red as a tomato.

'How was Mallorca then?'

'. . . Shit. Got Covid.'

I laugh. It hurts.

'Don't laugh, babe,' Her hand stays in mine.

'I found a new flat, you know. But it's too big for one, so –'

'But I haven't got a job.'

'You'll find something,' she smiles. 'You always do.'

And next to her. There's . . .

'Mum.'

Face chalked with tears.

'I'm sorry, Rainer,' she says, taking my hand.

'What for?'

'I don't know . . . but I want to.'

She strokes my face, eyes soft for once. 'There's someone else coming.'

'Who?'

I cough and it makes my ribs hurt. Nadia quickly clears the room.

Skyler squeaks, as she leaves, 'I'll grab you a Snickers, Oh!'

She hurtles back, 'check your phone: you got mail!'

And indeed I do. Phone on the side throbs blue.

An email . . . from. . . .

No.

'Dear Rainer. We have read your work with great interest.'

What?

'We're a small publisher but we're ambitious and we'd love to talk to you about your book.'

What!

'We think you really have something.'

'I have something, Skyler, did you hear? I –'

But she's gone.

Only Nadia.

She takes my phone. Dims the light.

'Why?'

'It's nicer, no?'

And it was. White lights stream through the dark window, traffic curling round the walls.

'Rainer –'

. . . Nadia whispers.

'You have to tell us. You have to say it out loud. Or it will never be true.'

Below the window, the river is blue. My throat clings.

Out on the bridge, at the bus-stop, ever so faintly. Is a man. It's him. His grey coat, flapping.

'But then . . .' eyes sting . . . 'then he'll be gone.'

'. . . No,' she smiles, 'just further away.'

She turns to the audience.

I'm really sorry. But I lied to you all.

Dad, see, he was . . . um, never famous.

And he didn't . . .

Die slowly.

He died quickly. On a hot summer's day.

I found him in that room.

Hanging from a hook.

Like his coat, on the door.

A bus squeals past in the night. The man holds out his hand to stop it.

He told me he was gonna do it. But I never told anyone.

'Why?'

Because . . . I couldn't believe . . . that he could . . . –

It was my fault.

'It wasn't . . .' Nadia whispers. 'He would've done it anyway. In the end.'

Maybe she's right.

I look back to the bridge. The man has gone. The bus gently drifts away.

But on the other side, an Angel rides by.

Head bent forward, charging through the dark.

Her box clamped on like a turtle.

This play doesn't really have a message. I don't want you to burn everything down.

I just want . . . you to see her. That Angel. Crossing the bridge.

Or that guy at Tescos, half asleep.

Or the drunks at the pub.

The Tuk-Tuk, wailing DnB.

See them.

See History.

Sludgy, broken, re-built.

To ghosts, dancing by the Lambeth docks.

To big steel towers.

To spaceships.

To Tinder dates gone wrong. See them.

To the two girls crossing the bridge. Bacardis and fags. Screaming up to the night.

I . . . love you.

I love you.

She turns to the audience.

And all of you, too.

. . . A knock at the door.

A knock at the door.

'It's open, Skyler!'

One more thing, before she comes in.

That guy, Jack?

Another knock.

'Skyler, it's open!'

The door creaks behind.

He never ghosted me.

I ghosted him.

'Rainer.'

Cos anything good in my life just drifts, drifts away.

'Rainer –'

It drifts away.

'Did you get the Snickers, then?'

I turn around. Eyes adjusting to the dark.

'Skyler?'

. . . But no.

No Skyler.

No Snickers.

But him.

His pretty face, smiling in the dark.

He holds his hand out.

But I freeze. Pale.

I hear Nadia's voice,

'Rainer . . .

'What?'

'. . . You need to let people in.'

. . . He takes a step forward.

And another . . .

. . . And so do I.

I hold a hand up. To his pretty little face.

'Hello, Rainer.'

'. . . Hello, Jack.'

. . .

And I hold him.

. . .

Like a cat.

End.

9 781350 350922